Seek Until You're Astonished

WALTER & MAE —

Blessed to have met you.

Honored to now call you Friends.

Look for the good

Ron

Seek Until You're Astonished

*Finding the Mystery of God
in the Question*

Ron Fritts

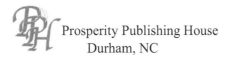
Prosperity Publishing House
Durham, NC

This publication is designed to provide accurate and authoritative information in regard to the subject matter covered. It is sold with the understanding that the publisher is not engaged in rendering legal, accounting, or other professional service. If legal advice or other expert assistance is required, the services of a competent professional person should be sought. (From a Declaration of Principles jointly adopted by a Committee of the American Bar Association and a Committee of Publishers).

Prosperity Publishing House
   Durham, NC

Library of Congress Cataloging-in-Publication Data

Fritts, Ron
Seek Until You're Astonished / Ron Fritts
p. cm.

ISBN 978-1-946291-27-1 (Print-softcover)
ISBN 978-1-946291-28-8 (Kindle)
ISBN 978-1-946291-29-5 (Ebook)

   1. Spiritual   2. New Thought   3. Self Help
   II. Title

Library of Congress Control Number: 2023914664
Printed in the United States of America

10 9 8 7 6 5 4 3 2 1

"Jesus said: The seeker should not stop until he finds. When he does find, he will be disturbed. After having been disturbed, he will be astonished. Then he will reign over everything."

~ The Gospel of Thomas, translated by Stevan Davies

I dedicate this book to my mother, who taught me with her words and modeled through her actions the importance of questioning and the joy of being astonished.

Table of Contents

Are There No Answers?

Are There No Answers?

"No one is dumb who is curious. The people who don't ask questions remain clueless throughout their lives."
~ *Neil deGrasse Tyson*

"Any belief that does not stand up to questioning is a belief not worth believing in."
~ *Bil & Cher Holton*

I have come to value silence/quiet time. Sometimes this is the goal of meditation, a place of mindlessness (which I will talk more about in the last chapter). But whether it's labeled meditation or not, the silence is where I connect with God, spirit, the universe, my higher self or whatever you want to call it. It is a place where it feels safe to question, to rest into being open to ideas and beliefs, or to just be content with what is.

As you begin reading, I invite you into a few moments of silence. It need not be long, just a minute or two. But as you close your eyes, concentrate on opening your mind and heart. Know that there will be no coercion, no pressure to change, no judgement. Just be open to possibilities.

Now, let the questioning begin!

As long as I can remember I've been asking questions, seeking answers. Because of that, what I call my spiritual adventure has been at various times scary, exhilarating and mysterious. In childhood, neither my culture nor my religion encouraged questions. My parents were rigid about what I could and could not do. Church leaders were absolute about God, Jesus, worship and rules to live by. The Bible was God's Word and the only source of truth that was needed. Obeying and following would lead to heaven when you died and failing to do so was the certain path to hell.

You can imagine my childhood questions were limited, mostly because I never really thought about it. I accepted the answers. But in college and seminary I began to apply my questioning spirit to my religion. Why would a God of love and mercy need his only son to die before he could forgive me? How could so many people who differed with what I'd been taught be wrong? If God created me with this mind that questioned things, why would he expect me not to use my mind and seek answers? What if there was truth beyond the King James Version of the Bible?

Initially it was uncomfortable not to have the answer to so many questions. I think it was Bil Holton who, during some of our Think Tank discussions, first introduced the phrase, "question unquestioned answers." In fact, questioning un-questioned answers only left me with even more unanswered questions. But eventually I realized that living in that space was a joyful search and, as the saying goes, the point was the journey (the search), not the destination.

My wife loves to do jigsaw puzzles. Occasionally I help. I enjoy getting the border put together because it establishes parameters (and it's easier). After that she recommends finding a section of the picture to put together – a tree, a person, a house. Then comes the more tedious challenge of matching

4

colors and shapes. As you near completion, it's exciting to put those last few pieces in place, and finally exclaim, "Look! It's all done!" But then, you break it apart, put it back in the box, and start a new one.

And I realized, it's fun to start, and exciting to finish, but the real joy for her is in putting it together. This is what the spiritual practice of questioning has become for me. The curiosity that brings the question is interesting. It's great to find an answer. But that answer leads to more questions. And the fact that I don't know the answer is what I have come to think of as the mystery of God. But there is also the joy. I don't have to know the final absolute answer. If I can trust that there is an answer, I become comfortable in the space of "I don't know."

Over 4 decades ago, I was ordained in the church of my childhood, an evangelical Christian denomination. It seems like a different lifetime for more reasons than just being 40 years ago. After 4 years of college, a year in seminary and 12 years serving as a minister in several different roles and locations, I left that denomination, realizing I no longer aligned with that belief system. I spent the next 20 years exploring and wondering what I believed.

Today I am an ordained Unity minister. While attending a workshop at one of our national conferences, the speaker spoke of the importance of establishing a personal mission statement. What I came up with then, remains the case over a decade later "...to awaken and evolve; and to be a catalyst for others to have the courage, tools and support to do the same."

While Unity has been a significant support and bridge for me personally as I have evolved in my beliefs, this personal mission does not include a need to convince you to join Unity, one of the New Thought movements that came out of the late 19th and early 20th century. My goal is not even to get you to change what church you attend or to let go of your beliefs.

Rather it is an invitation to question your belief system and to assure you that it is safe and natural to do so. The best way I know to do that is to share my personal spiritual journey, which continues even as I write.

I consider myself to be more spiritual than religious. That has not always been so. But like most of us, I have been asking questions all my life. Questions about life, people, nature, science, God. Usually, if I got an answer from someone I respected or a book I considered authoritative, I accepted it. But eventually I began to question many of the answers I had accepted. What I discovered was how many things I had "accepted on faith," or more accurately, just never questioned.

> It has been a long and winding spiritual journey from the beginning of my questioning to here, with a significant wilderness experience in the middle.

This was more than doubting. It was being willing to ask, "Is that really true?" or "Do I really believe that?" That has led to a mental and spiritual adventure. This book is certainly not an autobiography, but it is drawn from my personal adventure, my own spiritual evolution. It is about the seeking, and the disturbance it creates, as well as the joy that can come not only from new answers, but from the mystery found in the questions. So, each chapter title is in the form of a question. And at the end of each chapter, I offer some additional questions to consider.

This is not intended to be a theological treatise. I am not a Bible scholar or a religious expert. I have been blessed to know some people I consider experts, hear them speak and read their writing. I have quoted some of them in this book. I consider myself a simple, but curious and open-minded seeker. I have written this book from that perspective. It is meant to be as if we were sitting in the living room or on the patio talking over coffee or a drink. A casual, yet serious discussion where we ask questions, share thoughts and explore together.

My hope is that sharing my journey will support you in your search, encourage you to ask questions and to be astonished and joyous in the mystery.

It has been a long and winding spiritual journey from the beginning of my questioning to here, with a significant wilderness experience in the middle. That journey has led to a myriad of questions, new answers (that sometimes led to more questions), exploring other Christian denominations, other religions, and the experience of not practicing any religion. Writing this book has supported this ongoing journey. As I have reflected on highlights along the way, it has led me to clarify my beliefs, sometimes confirming them, sometimes modifying. It helped me continue to "awaken and evolve" spiritually.

I have had the privilege of participating with several friends and colleagues in what we call a spiritual think tank. We question beliefs, imagine new ideas, explore possible alternate concepts. A few years ago, we led a couple of weekend retreats, inviting others to join us in the process. We called it, "Exploding Dogma, Exploring Divinity." It is an appropriate description of my spiritual journey, especially the last 20 years or so. If you have been questioning your belief system and are open to considering new possibilities, I invite you to come along on this spiritual exploration I am writing about.

These days I am still exploring, still questioning, but no longer uncomfortable with not having the answers.

I have met many people with similar backgrounds, whose childhood religion no longer served them. But leaving can create a sense of being lost, not knowing what to believe, even fear. And if you haven't found a belief system that supports you in your questioning, it can feel like wandering in a spiritual wilderness. I recall one friend who was a devoted Catholic for many years, who explored Buddhist meditation and other alternatives to his boyhood religion. He said the teaching of the church was so engrained in him, that to even consider another path felt like rejecting God. When he found a new construct that allowed and supported his search, it brought him great joy. And I was blessed to be a support and catalyst for him. If sharing my journey helps you in some way in your search for answers and new possibilities, I will be grateful.

Finding Unity has been a significant part of my evolution. It gave me the freedom to explore, offered some radical new beliefs, and supported me as I came to realize I was more spiritual than religious. I have heard many people in Unity express a similar feeling of "coming home" when they discovered Unity. They found a place of acceptance, openness, freedom from the dogma of their previous church.

But as I mentioned earlier, my goal is not to "recruit" you to become a member of Unity or even attend a service or workshop. It is just to encourage you to explore new answers and hypothesize new beliefs, knowing there are other answers and it is safe to question. It is to assure you that questioning and searching can not only lead to new ideas, but the searching itself can be a path of joy.

These days I am still exploring, still questioning, but no longer uncomfortable with not having the answers. Even as I have explored new possible beliefs, I have gotten okay with "living in the question." There's that expression, "It's not about the destination, it's about the journey." Well, I now enjoy the spiritual journey, even though I don't really know the destination.

I invite you to listen to my journey and if something in my story encourages you to ask more questions, I will consider this venture a success.

Questions to Consider:

- What are the beliefs in my belief system?

- Where did they come from?

- Is there a difference between a belief and an opinion?

- Am I open to new possibilities, even if they contradict my current beliefs?

The Bible Tells Me So?

The Bible Tells Me So?

"Over the past century an older way of reading the Bible has ceased to be persuasive for millions of people, and thus one of the most imperative needs in our time is a way of reading the Bible anew."

~ Marcus J. Borg,
Reading the Bible Again for the First Time

It was difficult to determine where to begin, but since perhaps most of my readers will consider themselves to be or have been Christian, and the Bible is what most Christians consider their source of beliefs, I'll make this the first set of questions.

As a child in the church I grew up in we learned to sing, "Yes Jesus loves me, the Bible tells me so." The truth is, most people in traditional churches consider the Bible to be their source for all their beliefs, even though most, I suspect, have never even read the whole Bible. If this is what you claim as your source, your authority, or your guide, I invite you to just be open enough to consider questioning some things.

As I said, I am not a theologian or a Bible scholar. To be sure, I have researched more than the average Christian. But if you want to explore what educated scholars who know Hebrew and Greek, etc. believe, there are lots of sources. I simply invite you to also ask questions and value your own innate wisdom.

While traveling once I saw a church billboard that read: "The Bible: Inspired. Absolute. Final." The only thing I could agree with was "inspired." Indeed, it is inspired and inspiring.

But absolute what? Absolute truth? Even if it were, it has come to us through so many translations, out of various original languages, that it raises the question of whether it's possible to understand, in today's English, what was originally written.

And it is surely not "final." It could hardly have been written as information or guidance for people thousands of years later, living in a world unimaginable to those of the time when it was written. So, it applies to us today only as we or someone else interprets it. To that point it certainly has value in its philosophy, its proverbs, etc. But why would that be the last information God ever sent to humanity?

Like all fundamentalists and most traditional Christians, to some degree, I once considered the Bible to be the Word of God, the ultimate authority. If not dictated by God to those who wrote it, it was certainly guided and guarded by God down through the centuries, so that it was the Truth, the answer, the way.

Gradually that belief eroded as I learned how it came together, who the writers were, when they wrote, how it was determined which of the many gospels, letters, epistles, etc. would be included in "the Bible," the process of translation to get it to the English I spoke. Think about it – it was never intended to be what it has become by those who wrote it. And the "source" itself has become a dividing factor even among Christians. It's fascinating and frustrating to think about how many different Christian denominations there are, and many of the differences have to do with how they interpret the Bible, e.g., the proper form of baptism, when and how the Eucharist/communion should be offered, the proper way to dress and wear your hair, etc., etc., etc.

The Hebrew Scriptures (Old Testament) include some history from the perspective of the Jewish people of the time. But their culture did not think of recording history for future generations as we do, nor did they have the means to do so. Their scriptures also include myths and legends that were an attempt to explain the world from their perspective and the knowledge they currently had. These were not considered to be literal, scientific explanations, but imagined stories. They most certainly were not intended to be passed down to civilizations thousands of years later. They had no concept of life continuing for thousands of years, and no possibility of knowing the discoveries that would occur over those centuries, which would completely change our understanding of how things are.

Simply put, it's not possible to translate word for word from Hebrew or Greek into English, so there has to be some interpretation of meaning.

The Christian Scriptures (New Testament) were written more like we would tell a story, give a sermon, or write a personal letter. As for the Gospels, obviously, there

15

wasn't anyone following Jesus around, recording quotes. We know that those who wrote about Jesus' life and ministry were doing so at least 30 years or more after his death and so were probably not even eyewitnesses, but people to whom the stories had been passed down. Paul, and the other authors of the rest of the New Testament, were also writing years after the events they were talking about. It is worth noting that much of the writings of Paul actually preceded the Gospels. Some Bibles include books known as the Apocrypha, writings not included with the Old or New Testament in many Bibles.

Reflect on things that you recall and share with others, that happened 20 or 30 years ago. Or listen to someone else talk about events that you were a part of. Details change, memories are different. Sometimes you think, "Is she talking about the same event I'm thinking of?" It sounds quite different.

Then consider that a group of church leaders gathered 300 years after Jesus lived and died, under assignment of their political leader, Constantine, emperor of Rome, to decide which writings would receive their blessing as authoritative and worth preserving.

Still, there were dissenting groups that felt important writings had been left out, so they hid documents which were discovered hundreds of years later. Only in the 20th century have we been able to read things like the *Gospel of Thomas*, the *Gospel of Mary* and other writings from the Nag Hammadi Library of the Gnostics. There is a belief that some writing was probably lost completely.

Those writings which were preserved and passed on as authoritative were in more than one language, none of which most of us could understand. So, it was translated into Latin, German and finally English, with the potential for error and disagreement about meaning each time. Simply put, it's not possible to translate word for word from Hebrew or Greek into English, so there has to be some interpretation of meaning. The first English translations are not even a language that is easy for most of us to understand, so it has been translated and paraphrased into our current way of speaking.

Here is just one simple illustration that indicates the challenge of translation and what the layers of interpretation over the years have brought about. In the Christian scriptures, the Greek word usually translated "sin" is hamartia which literally means "missing the mark." It has behind it an image of an archer shooting arrows at a target. He is aiming for the bullseye in the middle of the target. But, of course, she doesn't always hit it. It doesn't require retribution, repentance, or forgiveness, but training and practice. Isn't that quite different from what you have heard about sin?

> What actually happens unconsciously is that we go to the Bible to validate our beliefs.

The sacred scriptures of the Jewish faith – the Torah, and the Law and Prophets were originally written in Hebrew. Hebrew uses no vowels and reads from right to left, with no punctuation. Imagine the possibilities of interpretation that would be a part of translating that.

Additionally, I have come to revere the sacred scriptures of other religions. For me now, the Bible is two completely different collections of sacred writings for at least three different religions. Two of those, Christianity and Islam, have sacred texts drawn from the Hebrew scriptures. They contain some history, some wisdom, some value for daily living, as do the sacred scriptures of all religions. It is beneficial for our understanding of those two religions. It is worth consideration and reflection as part of my spiritual journey. But it is not THE word of God intended to be taken literally or used as the only authority for living.

I like Eric Butterworth's description of it as the story of humanity's evolving understanding of God and our relationship to God. Little of it is to be taken literally. Its value for living, awaking, evolving, becoming is mostly found in metaphysical or metaphorical interpretation. Unity's co-founders, Charles and Myrtle Fillmore and other New Thought pioneers had much to say about metaphysical interpretation of the Bible.

I recall one of my Spiritual Education and Enrichment classes about Metaphysical Bible Interpretation. As various verses were mentioned, I recognized the reference and could say, "Well, that's found in Psalms or Matthew." A classmate commented on how I really knew the Bible, but I responded, "I can quote verses and know where they're found, but I'm just now learning what they mean."

Additionally, what actually happens unconsciously is that we go to the Bible to validate our beliefs. I invite you to attempt a fresh, objective revisiting of whatever ancient scriptures are important to you and see if you can look beyond the literal. As a possible beginning point, I highly recommend *Reading the Bible Again for the First Time*, by Marcus Borg.

Questions to consider:

- What does it mean to say the Bible is the Word of God?

- Consider whether you believe the reports in the Bible are literally true? For instance:
    - Did Moses really talk to a burning bush?
    - Did Wisemen follow a star to Bethlehem?
    - Did Jesus walk on water?

Brainwashed?

Brainwashed?

"And the faith that grows out of questioning is stronger than the faith born of blind acceptance. It can withstand the shocks of circumstance. Only he who questions the universe and questions it in utter honesty can grow in his comprehension of the truth."
~ James Dillet Freeman, What God Is Like

We all have belief systems from which we live. From earliest childhood, we have been forming a personal belief system that includes opinions and beliefs that determine how we respond to people and situations. These may be religious, political, moral/ethical, or just functional as we make choices and decisions. But we always have a choice, even if we choose unconsciously. We hear ideas through our filters, our beliefs. We choose how to experience what happens or is said, and how to respond or react. And these choices are based on our belief system.

These beliefs come initially from parents, teachers, ministers, and other authority figures. However, the fact that our beliefs came from "authorities," or that the people who taught us loved us and wanted the best for us, does not necessarily mean those beliefs are true. People who loved and cared for us could only teach and model from their beliefs and opinions, which were also based on what they had learned from others. I like to call it Benevolent Brainwashing. I use the term brainwashing because the repetition of words inevitably impacts our thoughts and ideas. And one form of repetition that embeds it even more is music. (Think of the Christmas carols you can sing mindlessly.) But I consider it benevolent because these people were not intending to harm us. On the contrary, they wanted us to succeed, to be happy and in the realm of religion – go to heaven when we died.

This is summed up by a quote from Rev. Duke Tufty, in his book, *The Gold Road*. He says, "Problematically, many of the beliefs we are committed to underestimate our ability and hold us back from expressing our higher potential."

A Real-life Example:

My wife and I had attended church that morning with her parents. It was announced they were having a picnic in the afternoon. It was a carry-in, so like most of the church picnics I've attended, there would be lots of great food. And there was to be "entertainment." The food was plentiful and delicious. The "entertainment," it turned out, was a man who played guitar and sang songs that could have been sung in the service that morning and that were sung in the church of my childhood. Gospel songs, songs by a well-known group from my denomination. Songs that today I would never choose for a service I was leading. Songs whose words express theological concepts I no longer believe.

But a funny thing occurred. Even though I wasn't enamored with the "entertainment," I was listening politely, not realizing I was singing along on every word of every verse. My wife, who didn't know most of the words and had never heard several of the songs said, "How do you know all these?" And it dawned on me, they were so embedded in my memory it didn't even require conscious thought to repeat them. I had sung them dozens, maybe hundreds of times in church, prayer meeting, camp. I had selected the ones that fit the service when I was leading the singing. Repetition had stamped them in my memory bank. And I realized – I had been brainwashed, "benevolently."

Now the thing is, these songs weren't intended to harm me when I learned them. I wasn't forced to learn them. No one locked me in a room and played them over the speakers. In fact, the people from whom I learned them, who taught me about these concepts did so with genuine love and concern for me. They believed they were helping me, teaching me the truth, saving me from disaster now and in the hereafter.

> It takes a degree of maturity, wisdom, and courage to question our beliefs.

They were easy to remember because they had a catchy melody and a natural, poetic flow to the words. (Notice sometimes the words don't have to make sense, they just must rhyme. It's poetry.) Like Christmas carols, they were pleasant and felt comfortable, like putting on a well-worn pair of slippers. To sing them "unconsciously" (as I was that day) reinforces that comfort level. To sing them and think about what I'm saying reminds me that it is part of a belief system that is no longer mine. Beliefs that I now often find ridiculous, repulsive, or just foolish. But it reminds me that I once believed those things, and it's much easier to just "sing along," than to concentrate on a new way of being.

But we have the ability to change our beliefs. There seems to be an infinite field of possible beliefs. As we read and listen to other scholars, leaders, and authority figures, we may begin to question some of the beliefs in our original belief system. This may begin with doubting, but when it leads to questioning, we wonder, "Is it true?" "Why do I believe this?" "Are there other possibilities?"

Yet there is a human tendency to resist change. It takes a degree of maturity, wisdom, and courage to question our beliefs. I was in my late 30's when I discovered Unity and in my 50's when I really dove into the questioning of new beliefs and practices.

Most of us will not easily accept some radically different belief but may consider something that we read or hear that is similar to what we believe, that seems to make more sense. Blaise Pascal suggests, "People almost invariably arrive at their beliefs not on the basis of proof but on the basis of what they find attractive." Or as Steven Novella puts it, "We must realize that the default mode of human psychology is to grab onto comforting beliefs for purely emotional reasons, and then justify those beliefs to ourselves with post-hoc rationalizations."

This is an important process because, as Don Miguel Ruiz Jr. writes, "By consistently questioning our own beliefs, we open up infinite possibilities and avoid getting trapped inside a closed mind that only wants to be right."

Questions to Consider:

- Do I really have free will? Do I always have a choice?

- Am I open to beliefs that are different from my current beliefs, i.e. other religions?

- If God does not cause natural disasters like hurricanes, earthquakes, fires, what are other possible explanations?

What is God?

What is God?

"So who is God? No one can finally say. That is not within human competence. All we can ever say is how we believe we have experienced God, doing our best to expel our human delusions. Let me try to do just that. I experience God as the source of life calling me to live fully and thus to respect life in every form as embodying the holy."
~ John Shelby Spong

Bishop John Shelby Spong has been another bridge or support for me as I have changed my belief system. As a theologian whose belief system lies somewhere between traditional Christianity and New Thought, he aligns with many of my thoughts.

Notice my title for this chapter is not "Who Is God?" but "What Is God?" That's because for me, God is no longer a person, being, deity out there somewhere. Like me, you may have been taught that God was a "someone" (always a "he"), located specifically somewhere, with sort of super-human characteristics. The words and concepts used suggest alternately, an old man with a beard that may be kind or grumpy, depending on the day and circumstance; a judge that dishes out penalties for breaking laws; a teacher that "tests" us; a loving parent who teaches us lessons through circumstances;

or perhaps a kind of Santa Clause figure, handing out gifts to the good boys and girls.

None of those images were satisfactory for me; in fact, they were contradictory. The idea that "he" was a just God and required payment for our sins, but was also merciful, so he sent his only son to die a brutal, violent death as retribution for all of us, hardly made it more palatable. Those characteristics seemed like human characteristics that we were using to describe this otherwise indescribable being. I once heard it said, "God created man in his own image, and ever since man has been trying to return the favor."

As I gradually let go of those images, rejecting much of what I had come to believe, at one point I thought I was an atheist. But that wasn't quite true, because I still had a sense of something greater than my human self and existence. A better term for me, at that point, was a non-Deist.

God is everywhere present, in everything, but it's easy to become so busy with living, or to get overwhelmed by the news of things that appear evil, that we don't notice the Good.

An affirmation often used in Unity celebration services is "There is only One Presence and One Power in my life and in the universe, God the Good, Omnipotence." So, God is a power that is everywhere present and only Good.

I make a few changes in that affirmation, because I believe the words we use are very important (see the chapter titled "Isn't It Just Semantics?") In Unity, God is often spoken of as power, presence, energy, vibration, intelligence, and my current favorite – MIND. This broadens "our understanding of God to a field of love and intelligence, that is the foundation of the universe" (Ellen Debenport, *The Five Principles*.)

Let's consider some of these characteristics attributed to God in more depth.

Mind

At this point I continue to believe that humanity, the universe, and life in general are not pure happenstance or coincidence. I believe there is some source under, around, and within that seeks to manifest itself. While I don't see this source as a separate being and don't understand the why and how, I believe its nature is to create, to evolve. I don't believe this is something that just happened in the past. I think it continues constantly. I think we are not only an expression of it, but we participate with it, or as it. Like us, it may be in process, continually evolving. It is referred to in many ways. It is what religions call "God." Some call it the universe or energy or light. Let's look at some possible names and functions of this intelligence.

Presence

Another current favorite for me is Presence. I believe we can know and feel this Presence through nature, animals, and of course, humans. Let me share a real-life illustration.

A number of years ago my wife and I volunteered as foster parents. One of the children who lived with us was eventually adopted. But his adopted father helped us stay in touch. While I was attending a national conference, I received word that this young man, now 19, had fallen off a building and died. Since I was in a licensing program that required my attendance at this conference, I found the head of the program to tell her I needed to leave early to be home for the funeral. When I found her, she was talking with several other ministers. Her immediate response was to say, "Everyone join hands and let's pray." I don't remember a word she said, but I remember sensing the Presence supporting me in this difficult moment. On a side note, the lesson I learned from that experience was that in difficult times of illness, loss, or other painful experiences, it's our Presence, not our words that support and sustain.

Power

Omnipotence is redundant in the Unity affirmation I mentioned because it means all power. If there is only one, there is no other, no evil power (see the chapter titled "Did the Devil Really Make Me Do It?"). So, I leave that word out. "God the Good" sounds like good is a description or characteristic of God. But since the word "God" has all the connotations of the anthropomorphic being of my early years, I prefer to leave the word God out and say, "There is only one presence and power – Good."

Good

I hear traditional Christians, and even sometimes people in Unity use the statement, "God is good all the time, and all the time God is good." Nice positive statement, but for me it's not just that this God is a good God. Rather, wherever you see Good – that is God. If you follow me on Facebook, or have gotten emails from me, you know I use the phrase "Look for the Good." I often post stories of people helping others, showing kindness, etc. and include the phrase, "Look for the Good." God is everywhere present, in every-thing, but it's easy to become so busy with living, or to get overwhelmed by the news of things that appear evil, that we don't notice the Good. So, it's important to search for it and remain awake and alert to it.

Love

Another characteristic often mentioned in reference to God is Love. In the Christian scriptures (New Testament) there is a verse that says "God is Love." This is often understood as God being loving. Because I don't believe in a separate being, I don't think of God as being loving, but I think "God" is Love, one and the same. Therefore, anytime we see anything that is Love, it is God, it is the source that pervades everything.

God is not just loving, as if it were a characteristic, but is one and the same. In Christian scripture when it says, "God is love" I don't hear that as a characteristic of a being that we call God. I hear it as another word for God.

Life

Good is God, Love is God, and another term for God is Life. Life is present all around us in a beautiful variety of forms. People, nature, animals (especially dogs, ha ha). These are expressions of the Power and Presence all around. "Just as every tree is God in expression, just as every sunset or newborn child or act of mercy allows us to witness the divine, we too, are expressions of God on earth" (Ellen Debenport, *The Five Principles*).

Using terms like Good, Love, Power, and Presence eliminates a being with human characteristics. Yet to refer to God as a Higher Power doesn't quite capture it either, because that still suggests something "other than" me, something separate. The idea of Oneness means everything is One. Plus, if there is a higher power, it leaves open the possibility of another power, less than or different from the "Higher Power." But this Power, Presence, Love, Life, Good is all there is.

For some, this is difficult because it takes away the personal God that they can talk to and seek answers, solace, etc. For me, it has helped release a God that I was taught to worship, but couldn't even understand, let alone feel comfortable with. I have, however, "experienced" that personal God and there are times I still feel the need for it.

As Paul Hasselbeck writes in Heart-Centered Meta-physics, "Where Divine Mind may be realized as unfailing Principle, it is also true that Divine Mind may be experienced as a warm, loving Presence."

Even as I recognize that this Presence or Intelligence is not a "who," I can feel its closeness and know that through people, the nature around me, or within my own mind I will be comforted and find answers.

Here is a personal example:

My granddaughter was born with a rare genetic disorder known as Spinal Muscular Atrophy (SMA). Because of a missing or malformed gene, muscles don't get the needed protein to develop and stay pliable. The lack of strength in the rib area and abdomen make it difficult to breathe and to clear the lungs with coughing. So, they are susceptible to viruses and bacteria and can easily go into pneumonia.

It was diagnosed at 5 months old, and at the time the prognosis was she would probably not live to be 2 years old. Many children with SMA died before they were 1. When we first heard the possible diagnosis, we were hopeful the tests would prove different. We were praying, affirming health, and insisting something else would present as the problem. But the diagnosis turned out to be SMA.

This news came shortly after a retreat that I co-facilitated with a team of colleagues, and I had come away feeling I had more fully "released" my anthropomorphic God. I recall driving home and saying out loud, I suppose to "God," "Now who the hell do I talk to, who do I go to with my disappointment and discouragement?!"

The answer was mainly, other people who were caring, supporting, expressing it verbally, but mostly it was just sensing their "presence," knowing they were standing with me. Indeed, they were the expression, the experience of God. Also, my granddaughter was accepted in a clinical trial for a treatment that has brought tremendous improvement for her and many others.

Now there is another, even better treatment that she has started. She is 7 years old and much stronger, though she still requires 24/7 care. We are grateful, and her parents have become advocates for changes in school, the city, and other organizations. But it remains true for me that God is a mystery and an ongoing question.

Questions to consider:

- Who or what is God?

- Is God a he, she, or it?

- Where is he, she, it?

- If you used a different name or word for God, how might it change your view God?

Who is the
Christ?

Who Is the Christ?

"In him we live and move and have our being; as even some of your own poets have said, for we too are his offspring."

~ Acts 17:28

"...the mystery that has been hidden throughout the ages and generations but has now been revealed to his saints...which is Christ in you, the hope of glory."

~ Colossians 1:26-27

"If we've been kept from appreciating a cosmic notion of Christ up to now, it has not been because of bad will, ignorance, or obstinacy. It's because we have tried to understand a largely nondual notion with the dualistic mind that dominates Western rationalism and scientism."

~ Richard Rohr, The Universal Christ

The word/term Christ was, of course, not actually part of Jesus' name, though some passages in the Christian Scriptures refer to him as Jesus Christ or Jesus the Christ. In traditional Christianity, and broadly in our culture, "Jesus" and "Christ" are used interchangeably.

The term Christ, meaning "the anointed one" was added by his followers, and later, by writers and church leaders, long after he died. For some, that apparently meant that they considered him to be the Messiah, or the one who would lead the Jewish people in rebellion from the Romans and reestablish the Hebrew nation. It's interesting to consider the fact that neither most the Jewish people when Jesus was alive, or now, believe that.

AND, this belief led to some leaps to connect him to verses in the Hebrew Scriptures that were obviously not written referring to him. For instance, Psalm 51:1 says, "Have mercy on me, O God, according to your steadfast love; according to your abundant mercy blot out my transgressions. Wash me thoroughly from my iniquity and cleanse me from my sin." Knowing that this is Hebrew scripture, not Christian scripture, a casual reading would lead you to believe this clearly is a prayer to God, not to Jesus. But that's not even the case. The New Revised Standard Version explanation includes the setting for this psalm: "To the leader. A Psalm of David, when the prophet Nathan came to him, after he had gone in to Bathsheba."

This effort to connect Jesus with Hebrew scripture also led to equating Jesus with God as part of the Trinity, a term and concept never used in the Scriptures, but rather, a theological concept created many years later. It holds that God (the Father), Jesus (His Son) and the Holy Spirit are somehow all different, yet the same.

This partly grew out of the theological concept that humans are born in sin, destined for eternal punishment, and the only salvation from that is through Jesus, who was declared by the theologians to be "very God," even though he didn't make that claim. Some suggest that in John 1:1 the "Word" as it is translated in the New Revised Standard

Version means Jesus was with God from the beginning. But the Greek word translated as "the Word" is Logos, which means something like reason, idea or thought. It is a leap, in my opinion, to interpret it as Jesus. Jesus did claim oneness with God (John 10:30), but he also prayed for others to be one with God, "...that they may all be one, as you, Father, are in me and I am in you, may they also be one in us" (John 19:21).

For me, Christ is not a person, but a principle.

Another closely aligned doctrine views this person known as Jesus, as somehow 100% human and 100% God at the same time. Through fear and ignorance these convoluted concepts have been maintained by much of Christianity today. Some Christians would suggest that there is no way to "know" God except through Jesus.

Eric Butterworth in his outstanding book, Discover the Power Within You, describes what has occurred as the development of a religion about Jesus, rather than the religion of Jesus. For me, Christ is not a person, but a principle. Butterworth suggests it is "...a level of the particularization of God into man, the focal point through which all the attributes of God are projected into livingness." Christ is that of you which is God.

Franciscan priest Richard Rohr wrote an entire book about this word/concept, *The Universal Christ.* Some of his questions are, "What if Christ is a name for *the transcendent within* of every "thing" in the universe? What if Christ is a name for the immense spaciousness of all true Love? What if Christ is *another name for everything* – in its fullness?" He writes about the Christ as the Presence of God, as that which enables us to "see as God sees." He suggests it is present in all of us, indeed all things, but we lack awareness of it. He says, "Christ is God, and Jesus is the Christ's historical manifestation in time."

> The goal, the call is to follow Jesus, not worship him, to strive to express the Christ as fully and as consistently as possible, even if not to the same degree as he did.

This is a key reason why, if you ask me "Are you a Christian?", my response would be that you must first define the term. If by Christian, you mean that I believe Jesus was an enlightened person who was so aligned with or in tune with Divine Intelligence that he could do amazing things and change lives, then my answer is yes. If it means following his teaching, especially in terms of loving and caring for people above systems and laws, my answer is yes.

But if being Christian means believing the doctrine of the Trinity or that Jesus and God are one and the same, then I no longer accept those doctrines.

The goal, the call is to follow Jesus, not worship him, to strive to express the Christ as fully and as consistently as possible, even if not to the same degree as he did. Thich Nhat Hanh said, "A finger pointing at the moon is not the moon. The finger is needed to know where to look for the moon, but if you mistake the finger for the moon itself, you will never know the real moon."

I do not believe Jesus intended to start a new religion. He did not ask us to worship him. He discovered the Truth that was within, the Kingdom, his own divinity, and how to demonstrate it in his humanity. He points to this Truth for each of us and it is ours to discover and live it as well.

So, the answer to the question "Who Is the Christ?" is YOU.

Questions to consider:

- If I did not identify as a Christian, what might I call my belief system?

- How does it feel to think of myself as divine, or the Christ?

- Do I believe people I know are divine, the Christ?

Who or What Am I?

Who or What Am I?

"The difference between Jesus and each of us is not one of inherent spiritual capacity, but a difference in the demonstration of it."
> ~ Eric Butterworth, Discover the Power Within You

"Why do we care about the divine? Why do we quest and question? Why do we hunger to understand Divine Nature? For one reason: Divine Nature is our True Nature."
> ~ Linda Martella-Whitsett,
> How to Pray Without Talking to God

So, You are the Christ. I am the Christ. Like Jesus, we are expressions of God, Mind, Intelligence, Spirit. But, as Butterworth points out, this is not about diminishing who Jesus is or his significance, but elevating our status and potential. "…he who believes in Me, the works that I do, he will do also; and greater works than these he will do…" (John 14:12, New Revised Standard Version).

A number of years ago, there was a television series I loved, called *Joan of Arcadia*. The theme song was "What if God was one of us?" Joan was a high school girl, and God was the school custodian, who offered her guidance and answers to her questions. The concept was a bit edgy for traditional Christians perhaps, but for me it was a precursor for what I've come to believe. God is not just one of us, not just Jesus, but all of us.

Several things make this difficult to accept. First, we associate or identify with our mistakes in life. "The average person lives his life from outside in. He frustrates his potential when he lets his level of consciousness be determined by what people say, what conditions appear to be, what he reads in the newspapers....Then he is caught up in the dilemma of whether to conform to the world around him or to spend his life resisting it" (Eric Butterworth, *Discover the Power Within You*).

This is partly true because of the concept of Benevolent Brainwashing that I wrote about in an earlier chapter. We learn both good and bad, accurate and false from parents, peers, teachers, spiritual leaders, the media. This is not because they are mean or evil, or trying to test us, or don't love us. But because they, too, have accepted false ideas or old concepts.

Sometimes we believe these negative and limited ideas because of our own choices. The process of growing up in an imperfect world often leads us to a skewed, broken, or limited view of ourselves.

We are born Divine, Good.

One of the things we have been taught in one form or another comes from a belief held by much of the Christian world known as Original Sin. This is the belief that we are born sinners, or at least born into a human condition that makes it inevitable that we will do wrong, make mistakes, go against God and Good. This belief comes from a literal understanding of the story of creation in Genesis. (See the chapter, "The Bible Tells Me So?") In that mythological story, never intended to be an historical report about the beginning of the world or civilization, Adam and Eve disobeyed God and were put out of the Garden of Eden, and according to traditional Christian theology, all humanity as their descendants are sinners. Because of this sinful nature, we are destined to disobedience and sin until we somehow are redeemed from that nature. The theological term for this is "the Fall."

In a convoluted way, this story from the Hebrew Scriptures is then connected in Christian scripture to the story of Jesus dying on the cross. His suffering and death are said to atone for our sins and reestablish our relationship with God. This is necessary according to traditional theology because of this belief in Original Sin. Remember what I described in the chapter, "Who Is the Christ?" about Jesus being "very God," and thus, different from us.

My most significant experience of not agreeing with this theology was when I held my first grandchild in my arms minutes after she was born. Looking down at that face I remember thinking, "How could anyone think this is a sinner?"

That's not the truth of who we are. The Truth is we are divine, we are good by nature. The Truth is we enter this world with infinite potential and unlimited possibilities. The significance of Jesus is not that he atones for all our sins, mistakes, and screw-ups, but that he demonstrates the truth of our divinity and teaches us how to rise to our highest self.

In Unity this teaching or belief is known as Original Blessing, as opposed to Original Sin. We are born Divine, Good. When Jesus said, "follow me" and "come after me," He was saying, "Follow me into a greater awareness of the

Truth by which you can see and demonstrate higher and higher overtones of the law" (Eric Butterworth, *Discover the Power Within You*). But Butterworth also explains that this requires conscious, intentional effort on our part. He calls it the Great Decision: "We must decide that what we want most in life is to express the divinity within us." We must unlearn much of what we've accepted and intentionally learn and practice new ideas and beliefs.

> The good news is we always, always, always have a choice. We can feel beaten, broken, disconnected, but that brokenness can lead us to rediscover the truth of our Divine heritage.

The Buddha said it this way: "All that we are is the result of what we have thought. If a man speaks or acts with an evil thought, pain follows him. ... If a man speaks or acts with pure thought, happiness follows him, like a shadow that never leaves him."

The good news is we always, always, always have a choice. We can feel beaten, broken, disconnected, but that brokenness can lead us to rediscover the truth of our Divine heritage. It is often in these low moments, when we reach out for help, that God, Spirit, Wisdom, our higher self, shows up and reminds us of the truth of who we are.

Another way to think of our divinity is that we are Light. I love Matthew 5:14-16 in the Christian Scriptures, part of what we call the Sermon on the Mount, where Jesus says to the audience, "You are the Light." Indeed, we are each God at the point of us. Although on the path to learning and developing this truth we do many things that block this light and misdirect it, our true self is born of the Light that is God.

So, when my granddaughter was 3 years old, I taught her a different version of "This Little Light of Mine." We sang, "Tanner is the Light, she's gonna let it shine," and then we sang it putting in the names of each family member, the dog, and a few inanimate objects.

There's a card game that I love to play at the casino called Pai Gow Poker. One of the strategies a player can use is to become the dealer for one hand. Some think that changes the cards or the energy or something and gives them a better chance to win.

In her book *The Five Principles*, Ellen Debenport writes, "We are only beginning to realize that we are, each of us, the dealer."

YOU ARE the LIGHT, go and be.

More questions to consider:

- Do I believe in Original Sin or Original Blessing?

- What does it mean to think of humans as divine at their core?

- Can I imagine myself and others as expressions of God/Divine Mind?

Did the Devil Really Make Me Do It?

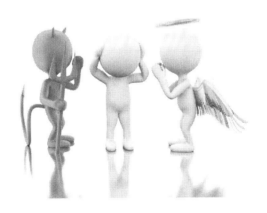

Did the Devil Really Make Me Do It?

"Deliver us from evil."

~ Matthew 5:13

"This, my dear, is the greatest challenge of being alive: to witness the injustice of this world, and not allow it to consume our light."

~ Nan Hua Temple

As I described in the chapter "What Is God?", there is only one Power, and since I do not think of that Power as a person or being, I also don't think there is another power or being such as Satan or the Devil. But I certainly recognize actions by people that are labeled evil. So, the big question is, what causes evil?

For most of my life I have thought of this phrase "deliver us from evil," taken from what is called The Lord's Prayer, as referring to God keeping me safe from the evil one or evil things. Or perhaps it was praying for God's guidance in my choices between good and bad. Either way, it came from the dualistic idea of two powers – God and Satan. Consider the possibility that it is a request or intention to let go of the idea of evil, looking beyond the appearance and seeing a different way of understanding.

The belief in an evil power seems at times almost stronger than the belief in God. I recall a book study I was facilitating. One person who was new to the theological concepts we were discussing seemed comfortable with the new concepts we were considering until I suggested that if there was only One Power and Presence, then there was no opposite power of evil. It seemed easier for him to let go of ideas like an anthropomorphic God or of Jesus being uniquely divine, than to accept there was no evil being.

This was when it started to register with me that in most traditional Christian theology, you must first accept that you are a sinner, separate from God. It is necessary to accept that one is either born in or destined to sin and evil, before one realizes and accepts Jesus as the payment for his/her sins, thus earning the right to God's mercy and acceptance.

> We can act in a way we call evil. But it's not because we _are_ evil. Rather, it is because we do not see the truth of what we are and the highest use of our power.

I would suggest that the reason we need a "devil" is that humans don't want to accept responsibility for their bad choices and actions. So, we want to blame someone or something as the cause. And then since it's "not our fault, or out of our control," we need God's mercy or Jesus' death to reconcile us. This is a much easier path than recognizing our failures and working at changing the way we think and act.

My current explanation for evil is that because we, like Divine Mind (God), have the power to think and create but are still in the process of becoming, we can misuse that Intelligence or Power. For example, my faculty of Love can be unconditionally expressed to everyone, or can be limited to family, friends, or like-minded persons, creating tribalism and nationalism, and leading to arguments and war.

Unity co-founder Charles Fillmore suggests this possibility in his book *The Twelve Powers*: "The electronic energy in man is a form of fire, which is represented by Gehenna. This electronic fire must be used unselfishly. If used to further the selfishness of man, it becomes destructive, through the crosscurrents that it sets up in the nervous system."

The founder of the Religious Science movement, Ernest Holmes, suggested in *The Science of Mind*: "The age-long discussion of the problem of evil will never be answered until we realize that it is not a thing of itself but is simply A MISUSE OF THE LAW OF FREEDOM … evil will disappear when we no longer indulge in it."

Another way to understand it is that this Power we call God is like light. Darkness is the absence of light. If you close the blinds on your windows, or cover them with black, the room you're in will be dark, even though the sun is shining brightly outside. Through the misuse of our Power, we block the light of divinity. Things appear to be dark. We can act in a way we call evil. But it's not because we are evil. Rather, it is because we do not see the truth of what we are and the highest use of our power.

59

Our inability to see beyond the appearance of evil leads to fear. Fear is a great motivator in traditional Christian circles – the fear of breaking God's laws and being punished. This is sometimes explained by the idea that we're not punished by God, but the law. We bring it on ourselves. To be sure, there are universal laws that if we choose to ignore, we will pay the price. For instance, gravity is a law. If you opt to step off the roof, you will hit the ground, and depending on how far down you go and how you land, you're going to be "punished" for ignoring the law of gravity.

The biggest use of fear in traditional Christianity is this acceptance of sin and the devil and the connection to eternal damnation or reward. Of course, in traditional theology that leads to the mercy of God, who is willing to forgive our sins. But again, for me, if this God is only able to offer this forgiveness because his only son died on the cross, that's not what I would call mercy.

It is interesting to note that in the Hebrew scriptures we find instances of God's mercy and forgiveness, and this obviously does not require Jesus' blood or death.

The longer I observe the inhumanity of humans, the more I find some of these answers are unsatisfactory or incomplete. Like much of my seeking, the question of evil is one I continue to "live in." But because I affirm, "There is only One Presence and One Power and it is Good," I remain comfortable with the mystery of the question.

More questions to consider:

- Is there only one power?

- If the devil/Satan does not exist how do I explain people or things that seem to be evil?

- What does it mean to look beyond the appearance of evil and see Good?

Could Every Thought Be a Prayer?

Could Every Thought Be a Prayer?

"Our words and methods of prayer derive from our sense of identity. When we view ourselves as "only human," we pray to God from a consciousness of powerlessness. When we realize our Divine Identity, we pray from the Divine Consciousness."

~ Rev. Linda Martella-Whitsett,
How to Pray Without Talking to God

"Prayer is creative thinking that heightens the connection with God-Mind and therefore brings forth wisdom, healing, prosperity and everything good."

~ Rev. Connie Fillmore Bazzy

One of the most significant changes that came as I developed my new belief system was how I prayed. Of course, I grew up addressing prayer to a God out there somewhere, or even to Jesus living in me. Pretty much it was in two forms:

- praising or thanking God for his blessings and goodness to me,
- asking for things, such as healing, help with a problem, getting a new car.

Let's explore these two forms in more detail.

Praise and thanksgiving

The idea of a God that expects or requires worship or praise brings an image of a king or ruler. That makes me a servant, child, or subject. Neither of those fit my understanding of God as Mind, Intelligence, Presence.

To be sure, an attitude of gratitude is beneficial. It changes your whole outlook, which then affects how you experience things. It opens you to expecting and recognizing the Good that is ever present and all around you. But I've learned that "thanks" doesn't require an object ("thank you"). I can just be grateful for every small and large blessing, including those things that seem negative or painful, which can become a lesson or guidance to something even better.

Asking for things

Even before leaving my childhood religion, this had become a confusing topic for me, leaving me with unanswered questions. A typical scenario is, "I have a job interview, all of you please pray for me that I will get this job." And I wonder – is there a formula? If enough people pray does that sway God to help me? Or does it have to do with the intensity of the prayers? Of course, this theology has a built-in, no-lose solution. If I get the job, God answers prayer, and if not, it wasn't God's will. This has numerous problems for me. There is the possibility that God is a giant puppeteer that controls everything that happens. Or the opposite – we manipulate or at least convince God. It opens the door for a fickle God that sort of toys with our lives, and that sometimes helps and sometimes doesn't. What about the other person that was also praying to get the job and didn't. Does God play favorites? How does he choose?

Let me share a quick example that illustrates my quandary. In our travels, we stopped one night at a wonderful hotel in an area that often had hurricanes. There had been one the year before that caused a good bit of damage in that town. The lady checking me in mentioned that most the hotels and restaurants in the area had damage, some so bad they closed the business. "But," she said, "this one has never been damaged. "God is good." And I thought to myself, "He wasn't so good to those other hotels."

Reflecting on my transformation of thinking

For a long time, before I realized how many points of transformation there had been on my journey, the primary one I recognized was my discovery of Norman Vincent Peale's *The Power of Positive Thinking*. I don't recall how I discovered his writings. It may have been Rev. Donald Dale in Colorado who introduced them to me. But however it occurred, it led to a major shift in my understanding, and to the way I presented sermons and practiced prayer.

It was while I was the pastor of an evangelical congregation that I began to read Peale's books and pamphlets. I became a financial supporter of his ministry and received their publication "Guideposts" which was, among other things, a great source of stories and illustrations for sermons.

I can't remember if I heard him on the radio, or saw him speak on television, but I was taken with the way he seemed to be in touch with people constantly – in taxis, at dinner, or at concerts. He drew spiritual meaning from everyday occurrences. Because of the impact of his ministry people sought him out, even famous people. He would help them make meaning of their lives, transform struggles into spiritual experiences without all the theological jargon that seemed required in many churches.

> ... a shift had taken place that would become the catalyst, the courage to walk away from a belief system that no longer served me.

Near the end of my ministry in the church of my childhood (though I didn't realize at the time it was coming to an end), I attended a conference for pastors in New York, led by Peale and his associate Arthur Calliandro. It was my first trip to New York City, an expansive experience in itself at that point. The conference was held at a beautiful YMCA retreat center in the fall.

The most significant part of the conference at the time was learning to speak without notes by using stories. The culmination of the week was attending Marble Collegiate Church on Sunday and hearing both of them speak. My approach to sermons changed dramatically.

But what I did not realize at the time was that a shift had taken place that would become the catalyst, the courage to walk away from a belief system that no longer served me.

A quote from Mysteries of Genesis, by Charles Fillmore, captures my experience: "It is by the work of conscious re-creation of his life after the pattern of the divine ideal that man gains self-dominion and becomes a citizen of the kingdom of the heavens, the inner kingdom of peace and power."

... the significance of prayer was its impact on the one praying.

Prayer is now quite different for me. One of the things I had struggled with for years was praying, especially public praying. It seemed to me that most prayers in worship or other settings were really addressed to the audience, not God. Ministers often seemed to be giving another mini-sermon.

No less troubling was the whole idea of intercessory prayer. How exactly was it that we affected God? Was it the number of prayers sent "up," the number of people praying, the intensity with which we made our requests? Of course, when I dared to move the question from my mind to my mouth, and speak it, no one had an answer.

In the church I grew up in, at the time of group prayer, everyone knelt around the kneeling bench at the front of the church. Those who couldn't fit there would kneel at the front pew or down the aisle. The minister would call on someone to lead the prayer. But within a minute or two of that person "addressing" God, everyone in the place started praying out loud. You could no longer hear words, just a din of voices. This would go on until everyone finished (or wore out) and it would subside until there was one last person or two finishing.

Peale's concept of the importance of positive thoughts suggested to me that the significance of prayer was its impact on the one praying. The idea of thinking positive was a shift, and "communicating" with God through my thoughts made sense.

> It's not about asking God to do things or give me things. Rather it's about affirming the truth.

Another aspect of prayer that troubled me was the "pray without ceasing" idea (*I Thessalonians 5:16-17*). As I read and contemplated Peale's approach, I began to see that every thought I had was, perhaps, a prayer. So, when my heart went out to someone struggling with a life challenge, I was praying. When I was captured by a breath-taking scene of nature and spoke of having a worship experience, I was praying.

My prior thinking about prayer seemed to cast God as either Santa Claus, doling out gifts (Have you been a good boy? Do you have enough faith?), or a super-parent figure determining what is best for me.

Everything changed as I was introduced to Affirmative Prayer, which is taught by Unity. It's not about asking God to do things or give me things. Rather it's about affirming the truth. Prosperity and joy are my nature. I can expect to have a job that provides adequate income and makes my heart sing. So, I can go confidently into the interview, knowing that if this doesn't work out, something better will.

I like the way Ellen Debenport expresses it in her book, *The Five Principles*, when she says, "In affirmative prayer, we are remembering who we truly are as expressions of the eternal life force on Earth, and we are taking time to align our thoughts and feelings with our highest good."

This affirmative approach can be a part of meditation, which is a good practice with many other benefits. It doesn't require words or someone else doing it with or for me. Among other benefits, this clarified the idea that first came to me when I discovered Norman Vincent Peale's approach – thoughts are prayers.

> Affirmations do not make something true, but help our consciousness to accept what is true.

As far as I'm concerned, the most impactful and helpful book I've ever read on the topic of affirmative prayer is Rev. Linda Martella-Whitsett's book, *How to Pray Without Talking to God.*

In a situation where we are praying with another person, Martella-Whitsett writes, "Do not think about prayer as a request. When asked to pray about someone's circumstance, think of the requester's intention – and name it a prayer intention. The intention, or objective, is to uphold the Divine Identity of the individual."

Affirmations are sometimes preceded by denials. It is not denying that we need help or need to improve or change. It is denying the power of our situation to control us. It is not denial of what we are experiencing, like denying that it's raining and I'm getting wet, but denying that the rain has the power to ruin my day. It is to declare something false and is often followed by affirming something that is true.

New Thought writer Emile Cady says, "To affirm anything is to assert positively that it is so, even in the face of all contrary evidence." Affirmations do not make something true, but help our consciousness to accept what is true.

Examples of Denials:
- There is no evil.
- There is no absence of life, substance or intelligence anywhere.
- Pain, sickness, poverty, old age and death cannot master me, for they are not real.

Examples of Affirmations:
- God is life, love, intelligence, substance, omnipotence, omniscience, omnipresence.
- I am a manifestation of God, and every moment life, love, wisdom, and power flow into and through me. I am one with God, and I express those aspects.

This approach also changes praying "for" someone to praying "with" them. When I'm finding it difficult to remember the truth about my nature, when I'm struggling to affirm the good, you can hold it for me/with me in your consciousness. Again, this is not so much about the right words, as it is about thoughts and Presence.

If you recall the story about our foster child dying suddenly in the chapter "What Is God?," I did not remember who else was in the circle or what words were spoken, but I recall vividly the sense that all was well, despite my situation.

I'd like to end this chapter with a song written by Lucille Olsen., whose beautiful music is sung by New Thought churches all over the United States and Canada. This particular piece captures the essence of my message about prayer.

Our Thoughts Are Prayers

Words and Music by Lucille Olson

Our thoughts are prayers, and we are always praying.
Our thoughts are prayers, take charge of what you're
  saying.
Seek a higher consciousness, a state of peacefulness,
And know that God is always there
And every thought becomes a prayer.

Our thoughts are prayers, the tools that we create with.
Our thoughts are prayers that Spirit resonates with.
Seek a higher consciousness, a state of mindfulness,
And know that God is always there,
And every thought becomes a prayer.

More questions to consider:

- How does prayer change things?

- Is every thought is a prayer, how does that impact my thoughts?

Am I a
Christian?

Am I a Christian?

"As you evolve you will make a lot of people uncom-
fortable. Evolve anyway. "

~ *Pauline Nguyen*

If you've hung in there with me this far, your question at this point might be, "So, are you a Christian?" For me to answer that requires some mental interpretation, somewhat like previous questions I've addressed: "What is God?" and "Who is the Christ?"

Why? Because I believe how most people would define the term Christian no longer fits me. If it is defined by following the teaching and example of Jesus as presented in the New Testament, I would agree. But, of course, that still requires further explanation.

There are at least two reasons why I consider this a question that requires a complex answer:

- First, I don't think most people really know in depth what their church or denomination believes.
- Second, they don't really question their personal beliefs or the teaching of the church they attend. They simply accept

what the minister, priest, Sunday school
teacher, or other religious leader says.

I did the same for a long time (see the chapter "Brainwashed?"). By at least seminary, and probably before, I had begun to question some of the teachings and beliefs from my childhood. There were discrepancies and contradictions, and things I was apparently supposed to accept on faith without questioning. I'll bet many of you reading this reached a point of questioning too.

> My current belief system is
> so different from what I
> know as traditional
> Christianity, and even from
> most Unity ministers I talk
> with, that I no longer care
> to be labeled "Christian."

My questioning continued without answers into my 30's, when I decided to leave the church of my childhood. But I continued to believe in something more, something greater. I saw positive values in the teachings of Jesus, even as I questioned the accuracy of reports about him.

Rev. Jim Palmer's words come close to expressing the doubt and frustration I was dealing with at that point:

I find it curious that practically every creed of the
Church, whether the early ecumenical creeds, the

78

Roman Catholic creeds, or the Protestant creeds are statements that outline the theological positions and doctrines of the Church, but hardly have any of the teaching of Jesus in them. Christendom is lost in a theological maze that has very little connection to or basis in the Jesus of history. Just for the record, Jesus did NOT:

- Start the Christian religion
- See human beings as "sinners"
- Die to rescue people from God's wrath
- Establish the clergy class
- Create a theological orthodoxy
- Write or read the New Testament
- Teach women were subservient to men
- Require people to worship him
- Say humankind is separate from God
- Tell people heaven is a future place
- Claim exclusive rights to God
- Encourage the practice of religion
- Believe in a literal hell
- Claim superiority to all other humans

Palmer sums it up when he says:

> Christianity is not the fault of Jesus. Jesus said the truth will set you free. If you are not free, you have not yet uncovered the truth Jesus referred to. Just because you are a Christian doesn't mean you have uncovered it. In fact, it might be the biggest reason why you haven't.
>
> ~ *Jim Palmer, Inner Anarchy*

I began to find answers in Unity and to this day have deep appreciation for the teaching and support I have received. I still consider my belief system to be founded on the teachings of Unity's co-founders Charles and Myrtle Fillmore, as well as Eric Butterworth and many more.

I don't believe in original sin. I believe our basic nature is good.

However, my current belief system is so different from what I know as traditional Christianity, and even from most Unity ministers I talk with, that I no longer care to be labeled "Christian."

Why? Here are several reasons:

- Traditional Christianity places more value on the Bible than I do (see the chapter "The Bible Tells Me So?"). It is considered the ultimate guide for life. Fundamentalists consider it to be inerrant and historically accurate. They interpret it literally and rationalize many of the contradictions and conflicts that creates.

  I consider it to be, first of all, two sacred scriptures: the Hebrew Bible (Old Testament) which is part of the Jewish religion, and the Christian Scriptures or New Testament. More importantly I view it to have value mainly as metaphysically or metaphorically interpreted.

- God is viewed by traditional Christianity as some sort of being separate from us, located somewhere other than us, and someone over us who gives, teaches, punishes, loves, helps, sends problems, and is somehow influenced by our activity and requests (though I've never had that adequately explained).

- Most who call themselves Christian seem to believe in some sort of literal, but other worldly heaven and hell. I do not. I believe we create heaven or hell in our own lives and world. I recall two situations when, in dialogue with friends, someone asked, "Where do we go when we die?" My answer then, and still is, "I don't know and I don't think anyone else does either."

- I don't believe in original sin. I believe our basic nature is good. I recommend Rev. Linda Martella-Whitsett's book *Divine Audacity*.

- Perhaps where I disconnect the most is with those who claim the title Christian is about worshipping Jesus as God. I don't believe we are to worship Jesus, as most Christians do, but rather we can follow his teachings and example. As Butterworth suggests, this is not to diminish Jesus, but to raise/empower ourselves to his level; to believe in our divinity, our ability to do as Jesus said, "all he did and more"; repeatability of the Christ.

    I once saw a sign in front of a church that read, "Jesus Loves Sinners." My first thought was, "Cool, I'll keep sinning so he'll love me more." But my serious thought was, "This is a reminder of a major difference in traditional Christianity and my belief system." (See the chapter "Who Is the Christ?").

- I don't view Jesus' death as atonement for our sins. I don't see Jesus as the only way to heaven.

I've known too many wise, loving Jewish, Muslim, and Hindu folks, and for that matter, atheists, to write them off because they don't accept Jesus as a personal savior.

So, if I'm not a Christian, what am I? I certainly consider myself more spiritual than religious. Like Charles and Myrtle Fillmore, I "honor the universal truth found in all religions." And I suppose, like Myrtle, "I am decidedly eclectic in my theology."

More questions to consider:

- What am I if I don't think of myself as a Christian?

- If my current belief system doesn't align with mainstream Christianity, how would I explain it to someone?

- Does it matter what label I carry or just that I evolve my belief system?

Isn't It Just Semantics?

Isn't It Just Semantics?

"Words mean more than they say. We have seen it again and again: Words can brainwash."
~ Lothar Schafer, Infinite Potential

"Words themselves are not the power but carry the power of the thoughts they represent. Words express a thought already held in mind. Therefore, in addition to changing our words to effect transformation in our lives, we must also change the thoughts which have inspired the words. The most powerful of all spoken words are affirmations of Truth."
~ Paul Hasselbeck, Heart-Centered Metaphysics.

These days, with all the talk about political correctness, cancel culture, and labels, you might think that the questions I'm raising are just religious semantics. But I have discovered that words and phrases not only express our beliefs, but they also serve to either further embed those beliefs or be a support in the process of changing them. And as I described in the chapter titled "Brainwashed?," when coupled with music, words are even more powerful.

Change Your Language

One of my spiritual practices is to change the way I express things to be congruent with what I believe. Some will say, "I know what I believe, it's just difficult to change the way I've said it for years." Or "I know what I believe and what I mean, but I don't know any other way to say it." I would ask, "If you've been willing to do the work that has led to letting go of ideas and beliefs, and replacing them with new thoughts, why not do the work to find a new way to say it?"

Here's a personal example. The only way I heard God referred to growing up was as the father in heaven. Of course, that expresses at least two beliefs I no longer hold:

- God is male.
- God resides in a place different than here.

Even before I discovered Unity, I was questioning these beliefs.

Doing the work has been important because I have searched for and struggled with the words. This effort has helped me think through and process what I actually believe.

In a college or seminary class, I learned that the Hebrew word for God contained the idea of both male and female, which made sense. So, when early in my time in Unity I was introduced to the phrase, "Father/Mother God" it was easy to make that change. But then, as I let go of the concept of God as a separate being, and especially one with human/personal characteristics, even Father/Mother God was inadequate.

Using "it" wasn't comfortable. It felt too impersonal and separate. I heard other suggestions, like Spirit or Universe, but they weren't completely satisfactory. For me "Mind" has become an acceptable term, suggesting an Intelligence that is under or behind all that is, yet I am a part of it or one with it.

Now, when talking with others, I am comfortable hearing or using the word "God," but it's important to listen and express carefully, since many would hold a very different concept from mine. Doing the work has been important because I have searched for and struggled with the words. This effort has helped me think through and process what I actually believe.

> I say, "Everything happens for a reason, and you give it the reason."

Christ is another theological term that is fraught with meanings I no longer believe. In most cases it is spoken as a synonym for Jesus. The Christian Scriptures (New Testament) often use the phrase Jesus Christ. But, of course, Christ was neither Jesus' last name nor part of his given name. It is a term meaning "the anointed one" or the messiah, that was added by his followers.

In Unity "Christ" is used as the term for our true spiritual nature, or our higher self. But I have become very cautious about using it, because while it is understood in Unity circles, it is very different from how it is commonly used by traditional Christians and most people in our culture.

Changing our language includes questioning commonly accepted sayings. One example is a phrase I hear often: "Everything happens for a reason." Typically, that suggests there's a reason beyond our current understanding which comes from someone or something other than us. I once saw a sign on the street outside a business that read, "Everything happens for a reason. Sometimes the reason is you're stupid and make bad decisions."

I say, "Everything happens for a reason, and you give it the reason." It could be a lesson if you choose to learn from it. It could be an opportunity for you to pause and check in with your intuition, instead of just blowing it off and continuing the path you're on. It could be confirmation of a decision. But what it is not, is God or the universe doing something to you.

Examine Your Labels

Another area that must be examined is labels. We "name" something or someone by calling them conservative, religious, wealthy, outgoing, political, Christian, liberal, careless, crazy, etc. Subconsciously we think we know something about that person or thing. We, then, see everything that follows through that lens.

Asé (pronounced Ah-Shay) is an African word from the Yoruba language, which originated in the country of Nigeria. Asé means three very important things:

- Perhaps the most widely known meaning is a word of affirmation, like the word 'Amen' at the end of a prayer. It means, "Right on!" "Yes!" "I'm with you!" So, when someone says something you like, say Asé loud and proud, for it is definitely not a meek and retiring word. It is bold and powerful and affirms out loud that which resonates in your heart as true.

- Asé can also mean life force or life energy, similar to the concept of Prana in Sanskrit or Qi in Asia. Each person comes into this life with a certain amount of life force, which can be increased or decreased throughout our lives, depending on our choices. For example, negative thoughts and actions can decrease your life force and positive thoughts and actions can increase it. In the Yoruba culture, it is said that our Ancestors bring us the Asé. Those that have come before us have generated for us and leave behind for us a certain gravitas that becomes our Asé in this lifetime. Similarly, our descendants, those who come after us, increase our Asé as they help increase our bloodline and therefore our influence on this Earth.

- For me, the most significant meaning of Asé is the power to create that which you speak. As we've already discussed, Asé means life force, so it makes sense then that you are adding life force onto every word that comes out of your mouth. This is one of the many reasons it is crucial to be careful of what you are saying. It is imperative to choose your words wisely and intentionally. If you only realized how much Asé you have to create that which you speak, you would become much more aware of the words you add your life force to.

The next time you hear something that moves you down to your soul, the next time you contemplate the impact your energy has on the world, or the next time you wish to manifest something by speaking it into existence, finish it off by saying "Asé" with all of your Asé!

Questions to consider:

- Does it make any difference how I express my beliefs?

- Is there anything or anyone separate from me causing the things that happen to me?

- For at least one week, try being intently aware of the words you use when talking about God or spiritual beliefs and notice if it feels different.

So What?

So What?

"If you change the way you look at things, the things you're looking at will change."

~ *Wayne Dyer*

Putting this all together, what does it mean? How do I live?

Psychologist William James (who was a contemporary of the Fillmores) said, "The greatest discovery of my generation is that human beings, by changing the inner attitudes of their minds, can change the outer aspects of their lives."

Nobody is to blame for the notions we were given. Nobody intentionally taught us false beliefs. They didn't know they were false, so we believed them as our teachers and models did, and over the years we "proved" them to be true – or not. When we accept a belief which is false, it is cemented deeper and deeper into our subconscious.

So, when I step onto the tee of a par 3 hole, I'm not expecting to make a hole-in-one; I'm praying I hit the green. We constantly have thoughts and make statements that express the likelihood of failure or a negative reaction to what is going on. We have a Murphy's Law kind of thinking.

However, we have a choice. We can get off the merry-go-round of old thinking, false beliefs, negative responses.

Initially, for me, it meant recovering from the shock that I simply did not believe a lot of what I had been taught, and the difficult process of releasing them. So began a gradual process of releasing old ideas, concepts, beliefs. This process continues after many years.

Next was searching for a new belief system. I knew instinctively that I needed to fill the void created by what I had released. We all have a belief system. We live from it, usually without thinking about it. But the good news is we can consciously, intentionally change it and establish a new one. I suspect this process will never end unless I choose to go back to living without questioning.

> We must raise our radar or focus our awareness. That is why I have established "Look for the Good" as my personal mantra, reminder, spiritual practice.

More good news I discovered is that I did not have to adopt someone else's belief system, or any religious belief system. We can form our own, piece by piece, idea by idea. We can live from it, even as we continue to develop it. This requires the continued practice of questioning and releasing concepts and beliefs. It's also helpful to develop the practice of forgiving yourself for things you did and said from your previous belief system.

Then, it became a matter of following my innate Wisdom, my intuition if you will, and remembering that there is an intelligence, a Mind, that I am a part of and that I can rely on to guide and support me in knowing what to do. For me, that led to discovering Unity, reading, taking classes and eventually becoming an ordained minister (again, but very different). That was my chosen path. Yours will almost certainly be different from mine. Along the way I read other New Thought writers, including Ernest Holmes, the founder of Religious Science. Their churches have become known as Centers for Spiritual Living and as I write this, we have begun attending one where we live. I resonate with some of their belief system which helps in my continued exploration and adaptation of my personal belief system.

Some of my current beliefs may help you as you question and seek. Perhaps they will align with things you already believe, and you will know there are others who are like-minded. Perhaps they will assist you in forming new thoughts.

God is not separate from us, not a spirit that lives in us, not a light that shines through us, but One with us, and us with It. I am God at the point of me. You are God at the point of you. It took me a while to understand it, but I agree with Rev. Michael Beckwith when he says, "All that God is you are, and all that you are God is."

Because God/Good is the only real power there is, its Presence is all around me, within me, and expressing as me. Whenever I see and recognize a word, an act that is Good, it is God (see "What Is God?"). It doesn't have to be some grand act that everyone sees or that gets reported in the news. The smallest, daily demonstration, and the large, widely known acts are all God. But because our culture seems at times inundated with the negative, we must look for it. We must raise our radar or focus our awareness. That is why I have established "Look for the Good" as my personal mantra, reminder, spiritual practice.

Another word or concept that means the same as "God" is Love. Wherever I see Love demonstrated, it's God. Again, it doesn't have to be a large, magnanimous expression. It doesn't have to be something that fits into the standard, accepted definition of love, like the relationship of two partners. It can be the smallest offering of kindness to a human, animal or plant, or a compliment, hug, kind word, or gentle touch. It could be something big like the public proposal of marriage in front of a gathering or on a screen, the amazing response of people to help after disasters, the big demonstrations of Love – it's all God.

> To either blame or credit an outside, superior being removes responsibility from us as humans.

To paraphrase Paul Hasselbeck in *Heart-Centered Metaphysics*, I believe that Divine Will (God's will) is that each of us ultimately reveals and expresses the Christ or the composite Divine Idea, with Jesus as an example and standard for us to strive for. Then the Divine Plan is simply how each person decides to go about doing that. "Finally," as Hasselbeck writes, "Divine Guidance is the supportive flow of Divine Mind. It uses the amorphous Divine Idea of Wisdom emerging from one's Divine Mind to discern the road ahead and to formulate and implement the Plan."

All of this places significant responsibility on each of us. To either blame or credit an outside, superior being removes responsibility from us as humans. It places this anthropomorphic God that so many espouse back in the role of parent, judge, or Santa Claus.

If the questions and ideas I've shared have led you to be willing to question your own belief system and seek new answers, I will close with one final chapter containing some spiritual practices that may be helpful as you begin to accept responsibility for your beliefs.

More questions to ponder:

- If everything happen for a reason, who gives it the reason?

- How do I know what the reason is? For example, is it a lesson, is it punishment or reward, is it karma?

- How is my belief system or my life impacted if I don't believe in a literal heaven and hell?

Care to Join Me?
More Spiritual Practices

Care to Join Me?
More Spiritual Practices

"Your purpose, my purpose, humankind's purpose is to recognize, develop, fulfill, and actualize our innate divinity."

~ Bil & Cher Holton

As I said at the beginning, this book is about two things. First, sharing (and continuing) my spiritual journey. But more importantly it is about inviting you to consider your own journey, one that will take you into unfamiliar territory. It is not about joining me on my journey, because I believe every individual must follow their own path.

The important point is that I have arrived at a very different place in my thought and practice about God and religion, a place where I am happier and have a very different understanding of things spiritual. I refer to myself now as more spiritual than religious, a phrase I've adopted from my friends and colleagues, Bil and Cher Holton. It has been an interesting, exciting, challenging and sometimes painful journey, but I continue to explore and evolve. I share it in case others are searching or wandering in a mental or spiritual wilderness. I share it to invite you to question the unquestioned answers (another Bil Holton phrase), to encourage you to keep seeking, and to assure you it is safe and exciting to do so. I share it because I believe traditional Christianity is delaying or blocking spiritual evolution.

If you are interested in seeking, questioning and being open to new possibilities, here are some other practices that have been helpful in my seeking.

Gratitude

One of my current daily practices which has become very important to me is ending each day with gratitude. Right before I fall asleep at night, I reflect on what happened that day for which I'm grateful. Sometimes this includes things that have happened in the past or things in life in general for which I'm grateful. The attitude with which we approach life is important, and approaching life with gratitude changes how I view things. Even though this is a practice I do at night, the thought carries over and I often find myself expressing thanks for things during the day.

Study

A valuable practice for me has been study and discussion through books and classes. Stephen Johnson, in his book *Where Do Good Ideas Come From,* suggests the best ideas come in a "coffeehouse" environment. How about that Baby Boomers? We had the right idea years ago.

Practice the Presence - Listening

One of my most recent practices has been to attempt to be more and more "present to the present." Not focused on yesterday or tomorrow, either bemoaning mistakes or remembering positive experiences or planning and anticipating what's next, but more attuned to whatever I am seeing, hearing, experiencing in this moment.

This is not to devalue what can be learned from the past. Mistakes and unpleasant experiences can be motivators for change. The joy of past experiences can be a very pleasant memory, a sort of re-living of blessings, celebrations, and accomplishments. It is not to discount dreaming and planning, which are necessary and can lead to even better future experiences and accomplishments. But it is true that the past is gone, and the future never comes, so the present moment is where we live.

This realization has several facets for me. It is the way to fully experience what is happening. Remember, we create the way we experience things. I don't cause or control things that happen, but I always have a choice as to how I experience and how I respond to them.

Another facet of this practice is a gift to others. Listening, without trying to give answers or solutions, is an important part of this practice. One of the things I learned from serving as a minister was that when people were experiencing crisis, illness, or grief, simply being present was what I could offer. So often when trying to "minister" or just befriend someone, words seemed powerless to comfort or bolster their spirit. But just being there with them was appreciated.

Remembering times when I have dealt with difficult or painful experiences, it has been so helpful to know others were thinking of me (thoughts are prayers). I rarely recalled the specific words they said, but the fact that they let me know was supportive. As I have contemplated this practice, I've come to realize that this is also the Presence – God at the point of me or you.

I Behold the Christ

Unity interprets the term "Christ" as a reference to humans being born divine – Original Blessing versus Original Sin. An affirmation that is often used as part of a blessing or appreciation to a person when they join the church or are recognized for a birthday or accomplishment goes, "We love you, we bless you, and we behold the Christ in you." That's how I learned it and often still hear it spoken in Unity congregations. I've changed the last phrase to "we behold the Christ as you." Can something so small as changing a preposition like "in" to "as" really make a difference? It does for me. ("Isn't It Just Semantics?") I behold you as the Christ.

Paul Hasselbeck introduced me to a practice that is powerful. You look into another person's eyes as you refer to them as Christ. Step by step you increase the intensity of the phrase until you address the person as "Paul, the Christ" or just "Christ." And, if you're like me, it's actually easier to see someone else this way than to see yourself as divine. I remember one of the first times I led a group in this practice. It was powerful when I called my friend Christ. But when she said it to me, I was moved to tears by the impact of the realization.

The point is to move beyond seeing someone as acting like or possessing a quality or characteristic and instead, seeing them as being literally an expression of it. To do this, you must first free yourself from the typical use of the term Christ as another name for Jesus. It was, after all, not his last name, but a title given him by the early church, referencing the Jewish concept of a messiah. (By the way, the Jewish religion does not view Jesus this way.)

After working with this practice a while, try looking in the mirror and saying, "You are the Christ."

The Face of God

There's a popular Christmas song called *Mary Did You Know?* It highlights the miracles of Jesus and the traditional Christian doctrine of his divinity through questions to his mother Mary. Did you know he would walk on water, give sight to the blind, etc. One of the questions is "Did you know that when you kiss your little baby, you kiss the face of God?"

Start with something easy: look at a baby. Maybe you have a vivid memory of holding your child or grandchild. When my children were born, I was so naïve and nervous that even though I was in the room when it happened, I don't remember much about the experience.

But when my grandchildren were born, I was relaxed and excited. All I had to do was wait until it was my turn to go in the room and meet them. The night my first granddaughter was born, I literally held her in my arms within minutes after she was born.

This was a particularly moving experience. It was easy to see in her the "face of God." It was a spiritual experience and I still see divinity when I look at her and all my grandchildren. OK, all children.

I know they must be fed and have their diaper changed. They wake you crying in the night. They grow up and cause chaos and headaches and worry. But start out easy: look at them in their most angelic pose – sleeping or smiling, and see if you can't imagine they are a physical expression of whatever it is you call God.

Then, move on to the bigger challenges of your lover, or dear friend, or mother. Don't focus on their physical appearance. Look at their inner beauty; see them as Love.

And when you've succeeded in viewing them that way, you can start working on those that aren't as easy to love.

Remember, this is a practice. The results, the accomplishment of seeing the face of God may take a while (like, say a lifetime or so), but the effort will be beneficial for increasing your spiritual maturity.

Meditation

There are a variety of methods and anticipated results for meditation. Some prefer complete quiet. I often prefer instrumental music. Others like a guided meditation that directs focus. This may include a mantra or affirmation of truth you want to embed in your subconscious, such as "I am Light, I am Love, I am Good."

One might focus on being mindful, being more aware of your surroundings, or concentrating on a change you want to make in your life. This can also be a time to ponder questions about beliefs.

I don't think it requires a particular position; the best is what's comfortable, perhaps not so comfortable that you shift to taking a nap. I try to remember that when my thoughts wander, I must not judge or criticize myself, but simply call my mind back to meditation. I remind myself that it is a "practice." While I may want to improve my concentration or extend the amount of time I meditate, I don't have to be perfect.

The Silence

Most often in meditation, I am seeking moments of mindlessness, an empty space in the silence. These words from a song by Jack Fowler come close to expressing my goal, so it is my closing remark. I invite you to quiet yourself and consider the possibility.

In the silence there is peace
In the silence there is unspoken joy
In the silence there's release
From a world full of chaos and noise.
So I wait for these precious moments
When I hear all that can never be said,
And right here in this Holy Silence
I find God
I find myself.

Credits:

Cover Design/Layout: Cher Holton

Images (Used with permission):

Cover: dreamstime.com/Aleishaknight | 15687798; canva.com
Divider: Pixabay.com
Chapter 1: 185397149 © Niroworld | Dreamstime.com
Chapter 2: 1267372 © Popa Sorin | Dreamstime.com
Chapter 3: 200802238 © Skypixel | Dreamstime.com
Chapter 4: 18357536 |© Cammeraydave/ Dreamstime.com
Chapter 5: 168502358 © Designer491 | Dreamstime.com
Chapter 6: 36480745 | © Agsandrew | Dreamstime.com
Chapter 7: 85056136 © Nicolasmenijes | Dreamstime.com
Chapter 8: 166076793 | © Alexandra Barbu | Dreamstime.com
Chapter 9: 78875013 © Robodread | Dreamstime.com
Chapter 10: 43169276 © Paul Looyen | Dreamstime.com
Chapter 11: 244720404 | © Designer491 | Dreamstime.com
Chapter 12: 38123606 © Luisrsphoto | Dreamstime.com

About the Author

Rev. Ronald L. Fritts was ordained through the Field Licensing Program, while serving as the minister at Unity of Quincy, in Quincy, IL. His introduction to Unity was when he served as director of music for Unity Temple on the Plaza in Kansas City. Upon retirement from serving as a minister at a local church, he worked for several years as a certified Ministry Skills Consultant for Unity Worldwide Ministries.

He served as President of the Great Lakes Unity Region and served on the Unity Worldwide Ministries Alternative Ordination and Credentialing Teams. Ron has a B.A. in Religion from Anderson University, and attended seminary there. He was ordained as a Church of God minister, and served congregations in Indiana, Colorado, Ohio and Nebraska, from 1969-1982. Before becoming a Unity minister he had a 19-year career as a YMCA Director.

Ron and wife, Cindy have been married 37 years and currently live in Cape Coral, FL. They have 2 children, a wonderful daughter-in-law and son-in-law, and 8 grandchildren. They have also been foster parents to 7 children.

His volunteer work has included being an assistant baseball coach for John Wood Community College, a Court Appointed Special Advocate for foster children, singing in the Kansas City Chorale, and directing the Monroe City Singers.

How to contact Rev. Ron Fritts for speaking
engagements or to order additional copies of this book:
Email: baseballrev@gmail.com
website: https://astonishedseeker.com

Made in the USA
Columbia, SC
12 August 2023

21410748R20067